AF454101

The Judoka Adventures

by Alex Panko

THE JUDOKA ADVENTURES

Published by Alex Panko, 2024

ISBN: 978-90-834308-0-5

Ready, set, judo! To all the little judokas, may your journey
be filled with laughter, learning, and lots of joy!

Meet your judo masters

Master Ji   Sensei Purple   Kuma-tan bear

Hi! I'm Tiri.

Today, Tiri felt a little grumpy. He went for a walk to find someone to pinch and bite.

As he walked through the city, he saw a sign for a judo school.

Judo?! Wow! That sounds fun!
I definitely want to try!

Easy-peasy! I can do it too!

柔
道

Hey, Tiri! In judo, we learn to be kind and respectful, so no biting, spitting, hitting, or pinching. Okay?

Come, sit next to me, and I'll tell you a story about judo.

Once upon a time, in Japan, it snowed all night long...

In the morning, young master Ji saw big trees that had broken from yesterday's snow.

But look! A little tree, shaking off the snow and standing up proudly. Being flexible is strong!

Ji loved this idea so much that he made a new way of playing - Judo, which means "gentle way". He built a school where everyone could come to learn and play judo together.

柔道

Many people came to the judo school, even Kuma-tan, the strongest bear.

Kuma-tan challenged Ji to a playful match, thinking that strength was more important than being quick and acrobatic. Who do you think will win?

The bear saw how fast and acrobatic Ji was and became his best student.

It's very exciting, but I really want to try judo now!

Okay, buddy! First, let's pick out judo clothes.

Judo clothes are called judogi, or also kimonos, or just gis.

What color do you like?

I like white, blue, orange, green, and ... all of them!

And I also want a red belt!

Beginners start with a white belt, but with lots of fun and practice, you'll get all the colors! The red belt is super cool because it's the hardest to get!

White belt

Yellow belt

Orange belt

Green belt

Blue belt
Brown belt
Black belt
Red belt

I'm ready!

Before we begin judo, we sit quietly and take a deep breath. It's called "Mokuso".

"Rei" is a polite bow to show respect.

"Hajime" is the command to begin!

"Matte" is the signal to stop.

Tiri did judo all day, learned new
tricks, and made many friends.
He liked it so much that he
decided to do judo often!

One day in judo class, Tiri asked: Can I be fast and acrobatic like Master Ji, strong like Kuma-tan bear, and have a cool belt?

Yes, you can! Just practice to get really good at judo and learn special moves like throwing and holding!

Tiri practiced judo for many days, and one sunny morning, he earned his yellow belt! But this was just the beginning of more fun ahead...

Judo rules for little judokas, inspired by Judo's Moral Code

Be Nice: Be kind to others and use gentle hands.

Be Brave: Try new things, like climbing a small jungle gym or saying hello to new friends.

Tell the Truth: Always tell mommy or daddy what happened, even if it's a little mistake.

Feel Happy for Friends: When your friend shares a toy, say thank you and smile.

Be a Good Sport: Play fair and take turns, whether you win or lose.

Stay Calm: When you're feeling upset, take deep breaths like blowing out candles.

Share and Play Together: Have fun sharing toys and playing games with friends.